Greek Sacred Sites

CORINTH
ST. PAUL AND
THE GODDESS OF LOVE

JILL DUDLEY

PUT IT IN YOUR POCKET SERIES
ORPINGTON PUBLISHERS

Published by
Orpington Publishers

Cover design and origination by
Creeds, Bridport, Dorset
01308 423411

Printed and bound in the UK by
Creeds

© Jill Dudley 2016

ISBN: 978-0-9935378-7-5

CORINTH

ST. PAUL AND THE GODDESS OF LOVE

From whichever direction you approach Corinth overland the acropolis of Acrocorinth beckons. On this high elevation, there was once a great temple of Aphrodite, goddess of love. Mariners and merchants sailing in from the west would have seen this landmark, before disembarking at the ancient port of Lechaion, about four kilometres west of Corinth. Those arriving across the Saronic Gulf from Piraeus, the port of Athens*, or elsewhere from the east, would have stepped ashore at Kenchreae; this is where St. Paul came c.50 A.D. after leaving Athens, where he preached the Gospel and gained two converts.

There were an estimated twenty thousand Jews living in Corinth at that time, many of whom had recently been expelled from Rome. At Corinth St. Paul stayed with a couple, Aquila and Priscilla who, though Jews, were Christian converts. Both Aquila and Paul were tent-makers, which was Paul's livelihood while he was staying there.

Despite Corinth's brutal sacking and destruction by the Romans in 146 B.C., it was by St. Paul's day a thriving commercial centre, the capital of a Roman province because of its geographical location, with many ships calling in. It was at that time a comparatively easy two-day journey by sea from Ephesus on the coast of Anatolia, from where Paul later wrote to the Corinthians warning them of the spiritual dangers of immorality. And St. Paul had every reason to be anxious because of the goings-on up there at the temple of Aphrodite, and the lax morals that went with her worship.

It would be interesting to know how much St. Paul knew about Aphrodite herself. Was he aware, for instance, of Aphrodite's own legendary love-life? Had he ever been told that tradition had it she was married to the lame god Hephaestus? Or the wild story of how she had had an adulterous affair with Ares, god of war? When Hephaestus learned about it, it is said he had cunningly created a net of spun gold, a net so fine it was invisible; then, when he knew his wife and Ares were having it off together, he threw this net over them and trapped them in each other's arms; at the same time he called his Olympian relatives to witness his wife's infidelity. The story goes that they all stood around laughing uproariously at the two lovers caught entwined together in the act of adultery. What an indignity!

Or did St. Paul know the story of Aphrodite's love-affair with Anchises, a shepherd on Mt. Ida, not far from Troy in Asia Minor, from which union she gave birth to a son, Aeneas? Later legend had it that it was Aeneas who was the true founder of Rome, not Romulus and Remus who were his descendants.

Aphrodite was goddess of love in all its complexities and variations; sex was something to be enjoyed, not avoided. St. Paul, on the other hand, preached about the love of Christ, the love of God, sexual abstinence and morality. He wrote: *Shun immorality. Every other sin which a man commits is outside the body; but the immoral man sins against his own body.* (1 Corinthians 6:18) St. Paul surely would have pursed his lips in disapproval at the sexual excesses that went on up at the temple of Aphrodite.

In its heyday the temple was said to have had no fewer than one thousand prostitutes to entertain the mariners and merchants who visited the city. The word 'courtesan' might be more appropriate for these servers of the goddess, because they were not only beautiful but gifted; they were slaves selected for their various talents in music and singing, bought only by those who had the money, and presented to the goddess in grateful thanks for some benefit received. One such example was an athlete who promised the goddess two hundred girls if he won at the Olympic games. He did win and kept his vow. Some of the greatest statues of Aphrodite were, in fact, modelled from these *Hetairai*, the girls who served the goddess.

In nearby Old Corinth where St. Paul lived and preached, there were numerous temples. One in particular dominated the city, the great temple of Apollo with its forty or so soaring Doric columns, of which only seven now remain. What did St. Paul know about Apollo? Or his twin sister, Artemis, whose temple at Ephesus had been one of the seven wonders of the world? Regarding the ancient Greek stories at Corinth, would he (a Jew from Tarsus, in Asia Minor) have known about Jason and the Argonauts, or Medea, Jason's wife? Would he have bothered here at Old Corinth with Glauke's Fountain close by Apollo's temple? Today all that is to be seen of it is a monolithic rock with two cave-like entrances into it. It was into its waters that the unfortunate

Glauke, Jason's new bride, was said to have leapt when she caught fire by spontaneous combustion after donning a poisoned garment sent to her by Jason's first wife, the wildly jealous Medea.

Or would St. Paul have noticed the Fountain of Peirene, so-called because a girl of that name had wept so much at the death of her son, that she had turned into a permanent flow of water? The fountain itself is today a series of arches over dark chambers with decorative pillars, and from the furthest chamber water flows over large stones before being channelled away. According to legend, the winged horse Pegasus once drank from this spring, and Bellerophon (a hero similar to Hercules, though less well-known) caught Pegasus there, and used the horse's magic powers to aid him with several labours that had been assigned to him. Pegasus was a favourite of the Muses and became symbolic of flights of the imagination. Had he known these stories, would he have been interested in identifying these places with them?

No doubt the answer is 'no'. St. Paul's mission was to bring the Greek mind from such flights of fancy, and harness it to his new message about the Son of God – the Son of the one and only true God, who had been crucified, but had risen from the dead. To be a son of a god was nothing new to pagans whose gods had often impregnated mortal women who had born them sons. That this Son of God had risen from the dead? Well, there had also been risings from the dead in pagan worship too. St. Paul wanted the Corinthians to realize that all such imaginative wonders were now past; their stories were fallacious, a mere preparation for the real thing to be found in the risen Christ.

Old Corinth was once a hive of activity of small shops and businesses conducted around its *agora*, the market place of Old Corinth. It is believed Paul preached his 'good news' from the *bema*. This was centrally placed on a raised colonnaded area where now only a platform remains paved with marble slabs. At the far end of it is a block incised with the words in Greek and English from 2 Corinthians 4:17: *For this slight momentary affliction* (life's difficulties) *is preparing for us an eternal weight of glory beyond all comparison.*

Kenchreae, the port where St. Paul had once stepped ashore on his journey to Corinth, was at the time a sizeable town. Today it is no longer a port, though in its horseshoe-shaped bay, the ruins of its ancient quay, and the remains of warehouses are still visible under the clear shallow waters along the shore.

From Kenchreae there was once a Sacred Way along which pilgrims would have made their way to Isthmia where there was an important sanctuary of Poseidon, god of the sea. Isthmia was located on the isthmus, the narrow strip of land connecting the bulk of Greece to the Peloponnese; this is now, of course, cut through by the Corinth canal, making easy access from the Ionian sea and Gulf of Corinth to the Saronic Gulf and the Aegean.

Maybe St. Paul on his arrival at Kenchreae, made his way along the Sacred Way; he might well have turned to look beyond the bay to the distant mountains of Attica and Athens, whose inhabitants had proved so stubbornly unresponsive when he had preached to them there.

Every other year Isthmia had held a Panhellenic spring festival at the sanctuary of Poseidon; at the time the Isthmian

Games were as famous as the Olympics and the Pythian Games at Delphi. The occasion would have been good for business for Paul the tent-maker. Pausanias (a second century A.D. travel-writer), described the occasion: *As you go into the sanctuary there are portrait statues of athletes who won at the Isthmian Games, and some pine trees in a line, mostly growing straight up. The temple itself is no higher than the trees; there are bronze Tritons standing on it. In the front of the temple there are two Poseidons, an Amphitrite* (Poseidon's wife) *and a Sea, all bronze...*

The Games consisted of foot-races, boxing, wrestling, chariot races, and there were competitions for musicians and poets. The winner of each contest was crowned with a wreath of wild celery, an award which did not go unnoticed by St. Paul who wrote wryly: *Do you not know that in a race all the runners compete, but only one receives the prize? So run that you may obtain it. Every athlete exercises self-control in all things. They do it to receive a perishable wreath, but we an imperishable. Well, I do not run aimlessly, I do not box as one beating the air; but I pommel my body and subdue it, lest after preaching to others I myself should be disqualified.* (1 Corinthians 9:24-27)

Today the Poseidon sanctuary site is a mass of tumbled column drums and ruined foundations. Only the Roman baths contain an exquisite floor-mosaic depicting Nereids, octopuses and fish in a swift flowing movement.

St. Paul's lengthy presence in the area, and his teachings, brought numerous converts; but in his absence trouble developed amongst the Christians themselves. In a letter which he wrote from Ephesus, St. Paul was anxious because he had heard reports that his converts at Corinth had broken into factions and were quarrelling amongst themselves. Regarding sex and marriage, he wrote: *It is actually reported that there is immorality among you, and of a kind that is not found even among pagans; for a man is living with his father's wife...* (1 Corinthians 5:1) He was upset because it was against even pagan standards of what was acceptable; unless Christians set an example of exemplary behaviour in their daily lives, what hope was there of pagans seeing the advantages to be gained by becoming Christian?

Constantine the Great (c.274-337 A.D.) was the first emperor to recognize Christianity as a true religion, but it was not till the early fifth century that the Emperor Theodosius II finally imposed Christianity on the people, and decreed the destruction of all pagan temples.

With the formal establishment of Christianity, the temple of Aphrodite on Acrocorinth was finally replaced by a church, and the sensual love of Aphrodite was substituted by the far more difficult-to-achieve disciplined love advocated by St. Paul.

It would be interesting to know what St. Paul would think of men today after two thousand years of Christianity. Would he be pleasantly surprised at man's humanity and self discipline? Or would he hold his hands up in despair?

* Denotes a separate booklet on the subject.

FAMILY TREE OF THE GODS AND GODDESSES

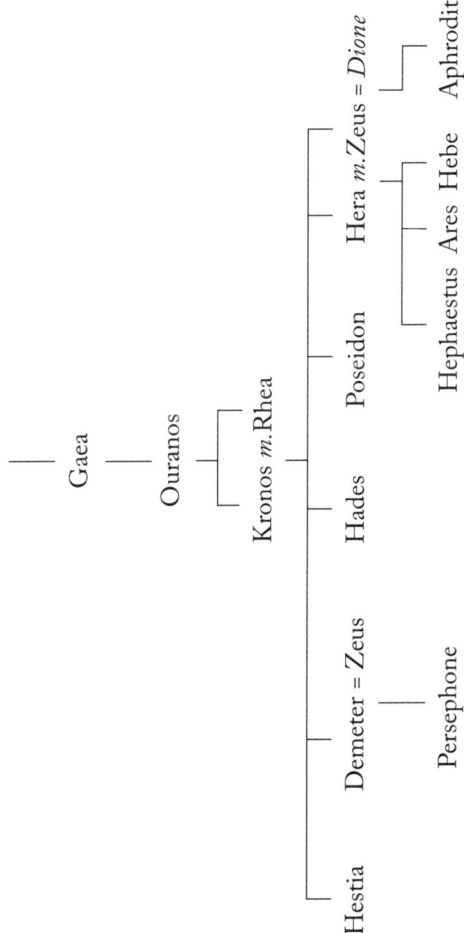

GLOSSARY OF GODS AND GODDESSES

AMPHITRITE – A Nereid (sea-maiden), married to Poseidon.

APHRODITE – Goddess of love. There are two stories of her birth. One that she was the daughter of Zeus and Dione, the other that she rose fully grown from the sea at Paphos in Cyprus. She was married to the lame god Hephaestus.

APOLLO – Son of Zeus and the Titaness Leto. He was twin brother of Artemis, and god of medicine, music, archery and prophecy.

ARES – God of war, son of Zeus and Hera.

ARTEMIS – Daughter of Zeus and the Titaness Leto, and twin sister of Apollo. She was goddess of wild life, and defender of the very young.

BELLEROPHON – He was either the son of King Glaucus of Corinth, or Poseidon. He was a hero similar to Heracles, and managed to perform several labours assigned to him. He also broke in the immortal winged horse Pegasus who helped him complete these 'labours'.

GLAUKE – Otherwise known as Creusa, daughter of King Creon of Corinth. Jason married her, thereby repudiating his first wife Medea who took her revenge.

HEPHAESTUS – Lame son of Zeus and Hera. He was skilled in metal-work and produced beautiful gold- and silver-wrought artefacts.

HERA – Wife and sister of Zeus, and mother of Ares and Hephaestus.

MNEMOSYNE – A Titaness, and mother by Zeus of the Muses. Her name means 'memory'.

MUSES – The nine daughters of Mnemosyne and Zeus. They were goddesses of the fine arts, music and literature, and such things as history and philosophy.

POSEIDON – God of the sea, of earthquakes, and also of horses. He was often referred to as the 'earth-shaker'.

TITANS – The offspring of Ouranos (often spelt Uranus, the heavens) and Gaea (the earth). There were said to be twelve of them, six sons and six daughters. Kronos was one of the sons, and Rhea one of the daughters. These two gave birth to Poseidon, Hera and Zeus, and several other of the Olympian gods.

ZEUS – Son of Kronos and Rhea. He was god of the heavens, supreme god of the ancient world, and dispenser of justice.

MORE FROM THE
PUT IT IN YOUR POCKET SERIES
GREEK MYTHS

TROJAN WAR
THE JUDGEMENT OF PARIS
HELEN
KING AGAMEMNON
ACHILLES
THE WOODEN HORSE
ODYSSEUS

ISLANDS
CHIOS – HOMER
CRETE – THESEUS AND THE MINOTAUR
KOS – HIPPOCRATES AND ASCLEPIUS
NAXOS – THESEUS AND ARIADNE
RHODES – THE COLOSSUS
SANTORINI – THE LOST ISLAND OF ATLANTIS

ALSO BY JILL DUDLEY

YE GODS! (TRAVELS IN GREECE)

YE GODS! II (MORE TRAVELS IN GREECE)

LAP OF THE GODS (TRAVELS IN CRETE
AND THE AEGEAN ISLANDS)